some do,
some don't

For my dear family
    —Dipacho

mineditionUS
An imprint of Astra Books for Young Readers,
a division of Astra Publishing House
astrapublishinghouse.com
Printed in China

ISBN: 978-1-6626-5095-6 (hc)
ISBN: 978-1-6626-5096-3 (eBook)

Library of Congress Control Number: 2022901202

First edition

10 9 8 7 6 5 4 3 2 1

Design by Amelia Mack
The text is set in Pueblito.
The titles are hand-lettered by Dipacho.
The illustrations are done in paint.

some do, some don't

DIPACHO

mineditionUS

Some of us have no family.

Others do.

Some of us take off on our own,

and some like company.

Others choose to stay put.

Some of us flee, never to return.

Others stay together.

Some of us enjoy a crowd . . .

Others like being alone.

Some of us live together,

even when we don't want to.

Others want to be near

but can't.

Some of us have families that seem . . .

let's say... different.

More of us than you'd think.

Some of us stick to our own kind . . .

And some find other types interesting.

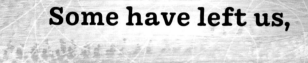

Some have left us,

and aren't here anymore.

Others just arrived.

Some of us fly off and follow our own path.

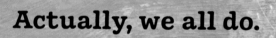

Actually, we all do.

A Bit About Jabirus

The birds in this book are called jabirus. The jabiru (pronounced jab-bee-ROO in English, or ha-bee-ROO in Spanish) is a large bird that not many people know much about. Those who do know them call them "the great stork of the New World," and not for nothing: the jabiru is the tallest flying bird in the Americas, measuring between four and five feet tall, with a wingspan of nine feet. Among all the birds in the world, the jabiru is second only to the Andean condor in size.

A jabiru has a white body and a black neck that is accented by a bright red throat pouch. The pouch inflates menacingly when the jabiru is upset or feels threatened. Although jabirus don't sing, caw, or screech, they communicate with each other by clattering their bills—and can be quite noisy!

Male and female storks look very similar to each other, except that males are larger. Jabiru couples build large nests on treetops, and they tend to mate for life. Both parents protect the nest and take turns brooding—that's when a bird sits on its eggs to keep them warm for hatching—and finding food for their hatchlings.

If you didn't know about this rarely studied bird, now you do!